Knowing You Have Done Your Best

No Regrets

www.KnowingYouHaveDoneYourBest.com

Angela Williams

Creative Team Publishing

Creative Team Publishing
Fort Worth, Texas

© **2019 by Angela Michelle Williams.**
All rights reserved. No part of this book may be reproduced, stored in a retrieval system or transmitted in any form or by any means without the prior written permission of the publisher, except by a reviewer who may quote brief passages in a review distributed through electronic media, or printed in a newspaper, magazine, or journal.

Disclaimers:
Due diligence has been exercised to obtain written permission for use of references, quotes, or imagery where required. Any additional quotes, references, or imagery may be subject to the Fair Use Doctrine. Where additional references, quotes, or imagery may require source credit, upon written certification that such a claim is accurate, credit for use will be noted here:

www.KnowingYouHaveDoneYourBest.com

The opinions and conclusions expressed are solely those of the author and/or the individuals and entities represented and are limited to the facts, experiences, and circumstances involved. No professional, psychological, or medical advice is implied, stated, or offered in any way whatsoever. You are encouraged to seek professional help, education, advice, and counsel from individuals you deem competent should you desire to learn more about human behavior, character traits, grief, insecurity, self-confidence, or a medically related topic.

Certain names and related circumstances may have been changed to protect confidentiality. All stories where names are mentioned are used with the permission of the parties involved, if applicable. Any resemblance to past or current people, places, circumstances, or events is purely coincidental.

ISBN: 978-0-9979519-8-1

PUBLISHED BY CREATIVE TEAM PUBLISHING
www.CreativeTeamPublishing.com
Ft. Worth, Texas
Printed in the United States of America

Knowing You Have Done Your Best

No Regrets

Angela Williams

Table of Contents

About This Book   9

Endorsements   11

Introduction   13

Chapter 1
Events and How They Were Handled   15
    Loss, Calamity, and Grief   15
    Endurance   20
    Coping   22

Chapter 2
Care for the Poor and Disadvantaged   31
    One Small Step (poem)   38

Chapter 3
Distractions   39

Chapter 4
Handling Complainers and Whiners   45

Table of Contents

Chapter 5
We Are All Extensions of God — 49

Chapter 6
Face Changes for the Future — 53

Chapter 7
Confronting Regrets — 63

Chapter 8
Forgiveness — 71

Chapter 9
Progress and Setbacks — 79

Chapter 10
New Beginnings — 85

Closing Thoughts — 91

*****

Credits in Order of Appearance — 93

Appreciation — 95

*****

Table of Contents

*****

Products and Resources   97

The Author   99

*****

About This Book

Knowing You Have Done Your Best, No Regrets is a book of resilience, survival, and growth, especially in the difficult times of life.

This is a book about choosing the highest, best, and truest courses of action even when circumstances are hard, or especially when things may not be going well.

This book calls you and me to look beyond ourselves and our immediate struggles, to care for those who may be less fortunate and disadvantaged, to honor personal dignity even more than someone's current station in life, to help others feel better about themselves in spite of differences, no matter how great or small.

This book questions how you and I face changes for our futures, and encourages us to make time to create value in ourselves, with no regrets, by exercising faithfulness and giving.

Knowing you have done your best, no matter what, is a refreshing way to live, where satisfaction comes more from correctly "being" as well as rightly "doing."

About This Book

We *can* be motivated by something, or Someone bigger than us, if we choose to answer a higher call. When we understand our responsibilities are to be resilient and to care, traits that must be lived not just talked about, we enter into realms of higher and blessed existence not possible unless we adopt this belief as real life, not just theory.

When we choose to place our priorities in correct order, we honor others' experiences and care for them, motivated by much higher goals than just personal protection, thinking and acting with just self as the major thrust.

In fact, we build ourselves up and do honor to us when we benefit others and reach out. This may be simple to state, often hard to do, but it is right.

We are extensions of God. We are called to fulfill His desires for us by what we do, not just what we say. In fact, doing and being are never apart; they are connected because we want them to be deep within the cores of our being.

If you want to confront life's ups and downs with improved perspectives, those centered far more than on just yourself, and personally benefit because you are growing in the process, then read on.

Welcome to my journey and life's lasting and beneficial lessons. Come join me, and let's learn together.

Endorsements

Patrice Borne
Clinical Staff Chaplain; VA and US Army Battalion Chaplain
Friend of Author

Angie … let me first say, "Wow!" I read what you shared with me several times … I couldn't put it down. I cried; I smiled.

It's amazing! *You are amazing!* In this day and age it's so refreshing to meet someone one that will go the extra mile in helping others.

Your heart shines through your writing! You exemplify the true essence of a heart of gold.

Your story is genuine, raw, strong, powerful, and hopeful. The great thing is that your story is not over!

Thank you for your vulnerability. So many will be touched and encouraged. Honored to know you!

*****

Endorsements

Duane Howard, Navy Seabee, Retired
Construction Mechanic 3rd Class Petty Officer (SCW's) USN

Author Angela Williams takes us on a path of self-reflection. She shows us the benefits of paying it forward and the value of emotional release. She describes how it is possible to selflessly sacrifice yourself for the betterment of humanity.

*****

Kathryn Woods, Friend of Author

Angela Williams is the real deal. Her life experiences and enthusiasm portrayed in *Knowing You Have Done Your Best* are beautifully illustrated and display a rare melding of memoir, experience, and the guidance of self-empowerment.

It is a must-read for anyone who has an inner desire to experience more passion, forgiveness, and fulfillment in their lives.

*****

Introduction

If you are like me, you realize that everything happens for a reason. There is always meaning behind occurrences, whatever they are. It is for us to discover what life's events are trying to teach us, and to then pass along what we've learned.

That's the reason for the book.

I don't claim to know all the whys of all that has happened to me, but I choose to rise above and do the right thing, regardless.

I choose the highest standards because others have taught me. My quest for lasting value never ceases, nor should it; we are all on a journey of challenge, improvement, joys, sorrows, hopes, and dreams. How we confront whatever we face is the truth-telling point for us, so let's choose better and best.

Real life is not a feeling, though it's accompanied by feelings, some good, some not so good, or some just downright ugly. Real life and love are seen in how we deal with whatever comes our way.

Introduction

I am not here to judge; I don't have that right, or that desire. I am here to present truths that have guided and helped me in the hope that you will be benefited.

This book is assuredly for "us," author and reader. It's my story, and is one that has certainly helped me grow.

So, enjoy, live, learn through experience and belief, grow, teach, and respond to a higher call if you are open to it and willing to accept that responsibility.

Chapter 1
Events and How They Were Handled

Loss, Calamity, and Grief

This is a big one for everyone. In my case it started on October 19, 1992 when my brother was killed on the job in a truck accident. My brother was driving what was called a gondola truck which kind of looks like a long open-ended dump truck about the size of a chip truck.

He was on his last trip of the night and heading home, when he came upon a small incline and corner, and his truck flipped on its side. What we can put together is an arm brace on the truck broke which hit the ground and this is what caused the truck to tip over on its side. The guardrail came through the window and caught my brother which threw him out of the truck.

When the truck came to an abrupt halt, the trailer flipped over the top of the cab and landed on him.

Yes, this was a horrible way to die, but we all prayed that his was a quick death and that he felt no pain.

Photo of the Cross nailed to the tree near to the location where Angela's brother was killed on October 19, 1992

My brother's death was a serious blow to my mom and dad and we pondered the ever-big question of *why*? Why did this have to happen? Why now?

My mother was hit the hardest as Tim was her first born, first grandson on her side of the family and yes, he was her favorite.

He left behind three sons: a three-month-old baby boy, a ten-year old and an eight-year old. Around this time his first wife started having mental issues, which was even harder on the older boys. They had just lost their dad and now their mom was losing her mind.

After my brother's death, as fate would have it, my parent's health started to fail. Mom had a couple of scares over the years, but the final surgery is what eventually would lead to her death. She went in for surgery and during the procedure she suffered a stroke while the doctors were operating on her. Following this, she remained in a coma for about two to three weeks until she finally woke up.

The doctors could not tell me how bad it was until she fully awakened. Well, she couldn't talk or move her right side. She was transferred back to the town in which we lived, about 180 miles away. She stayed in a hospital and was close enough so at least dad could go and see her. Eventually mom had two more strokes.

Now fast forward to August 6, 2005: my mom passed away. After she died, my dad really started to go downhill. Eventually his heart started to give him trouble and he finally wound up in the VA hospital for almost three weeks.

He was reeling from the loss of my mother, and starting to settle into the loss, but along came December 20, 2005 and my dad passed away.

Now picture the old TV series of the *Batman* show, and you see the BAM! POW! pop up on the screen. Well, I can tell you that's what it feels like: life comes along and BAM! POW!

Take that, and take this; oh, and just because you think you have a handle on it, KA-POW, a sucker punch. (That would be life playing a cruel joke on us). Now you are spinning like that boxer in the ring about ready to hit the mat for a knockout, and you think your world is about to come crashing down.

Photo of Angela's family taken September, 1979; Left to right:
Timothy Ray Smith (standing), Angela's brother
Loran Delbert Smith (seated), Angela's father
Angela; Juanita Faye Smith, Angela's mother

Knowing You Have Done Your Best

You thought I was done with all the drama? Well, you would be wrong. Now we are into March of 2006, and you feel like a zombie walking through life at this point. You go to the doctor and the doctor says, "Well, we found two tumors."

At this point, I am thinking, "Oh great! Now I am about to part this world and I have a seventeen-year-old daughter that just lost both of her grandparents and now she is getting ready to possibly lose her mom."

I always had in my mind that if anything were ever to happen to me, my mom and dad would be there to take care of my daughter.

Funny how nothing seems to play out like it does in your head.

> Funny how nothing seems to play out like it does in your head.

Thank God, it was nothing serious and I made it through surgery. All was good: no cancer, and none of the things that wildly go through one's mind.

So now you're thinking, "Okay, it's all good, or better." I thought I could slowly start to heal and put some sort of this chaos into a box and deal with it.

Well again, you would still be wrong. In November of 2006, my husband was diagnosed with Stage 4 colon cancer. KA-POW: a sucker punch again. This was life just making sure you are paying attention. My husband passed on January 3, 2009.

Now the question is, "How did I deal with all of this?" Well, you will just have to stick around to read this next section.

Endurance

Endurance: what it means to everyone is always going to be different. In my case, what I can tell you is that no matter what happens in life, I must keep going.

> No matter what happens in life, I must keep going.

There have been a lot of things happen to me over the course of my life: some good, some bad, and yes, even some about which I felt indifferent.

One could say, "It's that voice in your head…" Be it either your mom's, your dad's, or one can even say that it's God's way of talking to you in a voice that you recognize.

Knowing You Have Done Your Best

In my case, I hear my dad's voice, "If you can get up and call into work, you are not sick, let them send you home."

Sometimes we just have a choice in the matter; you must get up and do. I sometimes feel like a robot, or on auto-pilot.

There have been so many times over the years that I have laid down and prayed, "Okay, God, I am done; I cannot do anymore…" and yet I am still standing and still moving forward.

I struggle with this almost every day. There are times when everything falls into place and I achieve some small victories to keep me going. I have more and more victories now than I have had over the past few years.

We have all heard the sayings over the course of our lives, but let's be honest, because I can see the wheels turning in your head, "How does this pertain to me?" "You don't know what I have been through …" or, my personal favorite, "You are so full of it, you don't know what you are talking about."

And the ever so popular, "Why should I believe you?"

I have said all those things and catch myself still saying them.

I can only tell you what I have been through and what has worked for me.

Coping

So back to the question, "How did I deal?"

Well, when it came to mom, dad, and my hubby, it was all about them. Well, it was about me, too. To make sure, I had to stay sane through those few years.

This is where you get the strength for the endurance, the knowledge you have done your best, and you have no regrets. When it comes to you and your loved ones, yes, you can say it, "Be selfish for *you*."

In my heart, I know I did the best I could for them. I talked with them. I said what I needed to say to them, no matter how hard it was to say or hear.

I have had so many people say to me, "How did you do it? I would have given up or been put in a psych ward."

I would just smile and move on. Yes, I know it's different when you get even a small amount of time to be able to do this, like talk with them or be there to take care of them.

Knowing You Have Done Your Best

Some people don't get that chance, that closure, like in the case with my brother; we didn't get that closure to say what we needed to say or to be there.

In those cases, there is a lot of anger even when you do get some of that time.

It took me several years after my husband passed, to let go of all the anger I had. I was holding onto things that I thought would bring me closer to being rid of my anger, only to find out they were really holding me back.

> I was holding onto things that I thought would bring me closer to being rid of my anger, only to find out they were really holding me back.

I had been keeping this old recliner chair of my husband's. It was so worn out; it was being held together with rope. I still laugh at myself over it, so one day I was curled up in this chair and out of the blue it hits me. *"Why am I holding onto this?"* I thought of Butch (my husband), and how happy he was when he got it, and I got madder yet. Again, I was asking myself, *"Why?"*

It was starting to be little things like that, at first, that would make me upset. I would think back over the years of what I had been through, not enough time between mom and dad dying to deal with it, not enough time for me to get over my scare, not enough time with Butch.

By then I became so furious, I drug the chair outside and then put it in the garage to get used to it being out of the house.

I walked back into the house and there was the empty spot. The big hole; I just stared at it.

Now at this point you might be thinking, "She is bawling like a kid." Well, you'd still be wrong: I got madder yet. I couldn't stop being mad at them all dying. They'd all left me. They got to move onto a better place and I felt I was stuck in hell.

So let me tell you about the chair. This chair was in the garage, collecting dirt, and lord only knows what else. I snapped. I dragged it and another chair out of the house and into the middle of the yard and set fire to them.

While they were going up in flames, I screamed, "*Why!*" I hated that they'd left. I hated that they were being selfish. I hated that they could just leave and I had been left with this big pile of emotions and didn't know what to do with them.

I screamed at the fire all the things you want to say out loud but are afraid to because of what other people might think. Then it hit me: I wasn't angry with them. I was angry with myself for being selfish, even though I truly was not.

Knowing You Have Done Your Best

Now I stood there and watched it burn. I did cry, but not for sadness, but for relief from all the emotions I had bottled up, the emotion of being selfish, the emotion of being ashamed for feeling that way in the first place.

> I did cry, but not for sadness, but for relief from all the emotions I had bottled up, the emotion of being selfish, the emotion of being ashamed for feeling that way in the first place.

I know deep in my heart they didn't want to leave. They wanted to stay and be around to watch their grandkids grow up and graduate, get married, have babies.

But again, life never happens as we plan it out in our heads.

> I wasn't angry with them. I was angry with myself for being selfish, even though I truly was not.

"Saying Good-bye to a Lot of Anger"
The Chair Bonfire
Photo taken by the author, November 27, 2016

So, what I can say is this: find that spot, whether it is in the woods, at the beach, or alone anywhere, and just write down all the things you want to say but you don't want the judgement of other people, and scream.

Set fire to the letter, release it. You will thank yourself for doing it.

Most of all your health, mind, and soul will be thankful.

> Life never happens as we plan it out in our heads.

I have realized that coping with all that has gone on in those five years of what seemed like a kind of hell, was just life.

Knowing You Have Done Your Best

I have discovered that I am happiest when I am cooking. I crank up my music and I either bake or create a new dish. Now when I say bake, it's more like making fried pies. Now I just don't make a small batch it normally turns out to be about 250 + pies of assorted flavors, from apple, cherry, lemon, pumpkin, raspberry and raspberry and Bavarian cream.

Now, when I have a kitchen full of pies, I know I have to get rid of them. The only problem is when I create a new dish I have to have a guinea pig to try it out on. So, I give away a lot of dinners or baked goods.

Although I have known for many years that cooking made me happy, there were times through those five years when I lost my way temporarily. I withdrew from a lot of people. I just wanted to be alone with my thoughts, my anger, and my hurt. I needed the time just for me.

I didn't expect anyone to understand why I was doing it and frankly I did not care what other people thought. Every year I would take certain days off from work, regardless of how busy I was. It was always on the same days every year: August 6, December 20, and January 3. On those days I would stay home, unplug my phones, or turn off the cell, didn't go anywhere, and didn't talk with people. Those days I was a complete hermit. I would tell my daughter, Jessica, not to worry. I would be home and she would always know how to get in touch with me if she ever needed me.

Now I am not saying that kind of isolation is for everyone. Some people cannot handle being alone like that, while other people need the company of others or to just be out in the world.

I am also a firm believer in this: if you cannot stand to live alone, how do you expect others to live with you?

You have to find your special spot or place; some people call it their "center," or focus. It's a place of deep thought, meditation, or prayer. You will know it when you get there; that is for certain. It's worth the efforts you make to take that journey. It will likely bring you closer to God.

Listen to *your* heart, *your* feelings, and not what others are saying you should or should not do. They have their own ways of coping with sadness, loss, and anger that may be different than yours.

There will come a time when you say, "Enough is enough!" and you will just stop grieving or living in the past. Each of us has our own ways of coping.

Who is to say how long you are to grieve or be angry?

Just because you have finally reached that point of "enough" doesn't mean that you love the ones who have died any less now that they are gone. It just means that you

Knowing You Have Done Your Best

love yourself a little more than you did, and you are ready to truly let yourself start to heal and better yourself.

> You love yourself a little more than you did, and you are ready to truly let yourself start to heal and better yourself.

Chapter 2
Care for the Poor and Disadvantaged

So, remember all the pies and dinners I was talking about? Well, one day I was out driving about with my daughter, Jessica. We enjoy doing this every once in a while, and we hit all the second hand stores. I really love this time with just me and her, as we talk about anything and everything; it's one of the times we truly bond.

Well this one particular day we were at the Rescue Mission Store looking at some of the chairs for my next project to restore. Then it hit me—a true "aha" moment! I looked at Jess and said, "You know, if I should ever win that lottery, I would love to take over the mission restaurant." Needless to say, Jess looked and me and without missing a beat said, "Why do you want do that?" Now don't get Jess wrong ... she wants to make sure I wanted to do it for the right reasons.

My response was, "Think about it. Do you really think that every homeless person wants to be in that spot?" Now I know what some of you may be thinking, and don't be getting your feathers ruffled just yet. Let me finish the story.

Yes, I realize that some want to live this way. Whatever their circumstances might be, let's keep their choices in mind. It is not our place to judge.

So, let's go back to my "aha" moment.

If it should come to pass that I get to be in the position to help, and it may not be now or in the next year; maybe it will be when I finally get to retire from the federal government. I want to get in touch with the mission or maybe just open up my own restaurant for those who cannot afford a good home cooked meal.

Now what I propose is simple: if they wish to eat, all they need to do is help me out either emptying the garbage or sweeping the floor or washing dishes. I believe they want to be treated with a kind heart and to be given a chance.

Just one small simple act of kindness may or may not change a few or many, but what if it did? What if that one act of kindness helped someone take that one small step they needed to put themselves back on the right path, to love themselves, or to ask for the help they so desperately needed but for which they were either too shy or embarrassed to ask?

Knowing You Have Done Your Best

I know I don't like asking for help. Again, I hear that voice in my head (my dad's) saying, "Don't ask for help. That is a sign of weakness."

I have to say I am very grateful for that voice in my head. I believe it is the voices from mom and dad and the way I was raised that has gotten me through a lot of this.

So back to my dream, or the fight for a lost cause, you can call it what you want. I believe that we need to start helping people close to home, whether you live in a small town like I do, or in a bigger city. *Just start*. Again, every small step is one closer to the end goal.

> Start helping people close to home, whether you live in a small town like I do, or in a bigger city. *Just start*.
> Again, every small step is one closer to the end goal.

Like you, I see shows on TV or listen to interviews with big celebrities who make us think, "If I could just sit and talk with them, to pass on some creative ideas, to get that ball rolling…"

There used to be a show called, *Extreme Couponing*. It was called an addiction, describing those people who would spend hours clipping coupons and then stockpile what they had purchased for next to nothing. I am talking about the individuals who would shop and buy several hundreds of dollars of supplies and would pay less than ten dollars for everything. Talk about obsessive!

I would sit and watch, and think to myself, "Why don't these people contact the local food banks and help them out?"

Think about it: how much more could the food banks receive if they had a few people on staff who would look for ways to help supply more items, or simply just trained their staff on how to perform "extreme couponing"?

I truly believe that there is a solution for just about every possible problem situation out there. Our busy lives have got us so trained to focus on only what is in front of us at the time, through cell phones, television, work, etc., that we forget or just don't want to look at the needs on the side lines or in our own back yards.

Just imagine what could be accomplished, or how many more people that could be helped if we observed and responded to the obvious. It could be something as simple as getting more hygiene products to the homeless or for those who may need a small helping hand.

How many chronic health concerns and dangerous disease rates could be lowered or even possibly eliminated for those souls who simply needed a tube of toothpaste, shampoo, or even just a bar of soap?

Knowing You Have Done Your Best

Wow! Just think of the possibilities and potential results if everyone would just visit a local discount or dollar store and create a hygiene bag filled with simple items that cost little but could contribute much? For as little as five dollars, you or I can create one hygiene gift bag and drop it off to our nearest homeless shelter.

I know I can afford it, so I have chosen that this will be something I will be doing, starting soon. I know for a fact I have wasted more money than I care to admit on stupid stuff.

If I just rethink some of my ways of spending, I could make positive change. So could you.

> Just think of the possibilities and potential results if everyone would just visit a discount or dollar store and create a hygiene bag filled with simple things that cost little but contribute much?

Consider: if I put my spare change in a jug and once a month used that change to purchase and create hygiene bags, what a difference that action could make in others' lives that may not be as fortunate as I am right now.

> If I just rethink some of my ways of spending, I could make positive change. So could you.

Now with my new-found "aha" moment, I personally am going to be taking that first small step in helping, and just maybe I will get to my bigger goal of owning or managing the mission restaurant.

Like I have said, "It just takes one small step to make a change or create a positive difference in someone's life." It might take some time … one never knows. The idea may shrivel on the vine … but with a little love, this effort could grow into something bigger than all of us.

> "It just takes one small step to make a change or create a positive difference in someone's life."

So, if I am going to dream, I might as well dream big, right? Maybe I will become just a little less selfish, or maybe this initial activity will become the spark that ignites the fire on some of the dreams I may have been suppressing for so long.

What is your "aha" moment? Whatever it is, maybe it will begin to become reality for you and others when you venture out and take the steps to *do* something about it, even if you begin with small steps. If you act on your dream of helping others, you are one step closer to making that dream become reality. It *always* starts with that one first step.

That first step of action is like the little ripple in the big pond. It starts small but grows and grows.

Knowing You Have Done Your Best

Can you imagine your smallest act of kindness was the beginning of that ripple? Wow! The effects of it would positively affect not only others, but *you*.

> If you act on your dream of helping others, you are one step closer to making that dream become reality. It *always* starts with that one first step.

The possibilities of growth, strength, and most of all your self-love combined with loving others, know no boundaries.

You will find yourself becoming more empowered to become your true self, and you will grow in your faith and confidence to venture forth and try new things.

You will feel more confident when you help those who need *your* helping hand or an encouraging word. It may cost little but the rewards can be great.

> You will feel more confident to help those who need *your* helping hand or an encouraging word. It may cost little but the rewards can be great.

One Small Step

One small step
Can make a dream come true.
We can change our worlds;
It's good for me, for you.

Because God cares,
We help someone in need.
And we are blessed
In thought and word and deed.

~ Author wishes to remain anonymous.
© 2019 Creative Team Publishing.
All Rights Reserved.

Chapter 3
Distractions

I don't know about you, but this is a *big* one for me. There are days when no matter how hard I try, I cannot stay focused. Feel free to call it what you want: procrastination, distractions, lack of will power, etc. Even the strongest of people have those days so don't let them tell you they don't, because if they tell you they don't, they are in denial.

Now the trick is: how do you handle the distractions? Well, I don't have a magic cure or potion or exercise that will make them all go away.

Hey, wait a minute. This sounds like an infomercial. "If you act now, you too can have the cure for distractions and procrastination. Yes, you, too, can get all the tedious jobs done with a smile and eagerness.

"Are you tired for putting off jobs you don't want to do? Or maybe you have a co-worker, spouse, children or family members that are infected with the dreaded distractions or procrastination bug.

"Well, for three easy payments of $19.95 you, too, can have the cure. It's all organic, all natural, FDA-wanna-be-approved, and this horse pill can be yours!

"But *wait* ... there's *more*. If you act now, we will double the offer for the next 100 callers. All you need to do is pay for shipping, handling, and our processing fee, all for three easy payments of $19.95."

Well, that's the silliness that rolls around in my head when I get distracted. But not allowing distractions to rule is a very tough struggle for some.

I have to keep reminding myself of this question and its answer: "Why am I here?"

I am here to do a job by providing a service for our veterans. If I don't get my job done in a timely manner, it means that some piece of equipment or service may not be fulfilled when needed, originally designed to assist others to do their jobs in order to help our nation's veterans.

> I have to keep reminding myself of this question and its answer: "Why am I here?"

So, consider those people who appear to be either continually depressed or consistently angry, and complain incessantly in your hearing. You know: these are the ones who just suck the life out of you if you let them.

Knowing You Have Done Your Best

Those people could be family, co-workers, or friends. You may love them, but even these are the people you must distance yourself from, or take them in smaller doses, so to speak.

I have a few of those in my life. You dread that phone call or popup visit from them, because these people can become real distractions. I used to feel bad about cutting my time short with them, but not so much anymore.

It still comes down to self-preservation of mind and soul, at the least that's what it is for me. When these people zap your energy, it just makes it harder for you to stay focused in your daily life.

If you listen to them long enough, you may not want to do anything but lie around and feel sorry for yourself.

I think to myself, "I don't want to be this way!" So I start finding out what gets me motivated. I keep putting one foot in front of the other, and keep moving.

Some days are harder than others for me to discover the mojo that gets me out of my dark space, no matter how I got there. Over the years, relief and re-motivation have come from activities: some have ranged from cooking to reading or just listening to music. Occasionally, it can be that song that hits me just right. When I hear it, the feeling returns that I can conquer the world.

I start to get that little jig, dancing around the house like I do when I cook. I love to crank up the music and start cooking and dancing. This is my happy place, and I choose to go there. It's the place where my worries and stresses go away or at least diminish, and I experience a peace we all search for, though it often seems out of reach.

> This is my happy place, and I choose to go there. It's the place where my worries and stresses go away or at least diminish, and I experience a peace we all search for, though it often seems out of reach.

Ah, yes, it's the peace or focus we are all searching for. How to obtain it? That is a good question. How does one get to the place of not allowing distractions to rule and control?

I, for one, have to turn my cell phone over so I don't see it. I hide it under some papers; I turn down the ringer so I don't constantly check for text messages or the dreaded Facebook posts. The point is this: there will always be distractions in some form or another. We must find what works for each of us to get back on track.

> There will always be distractions in some form or another. We must find what works for each of us to get back on track.

Knowing You Have Done Your Best

So, I can make some suggestions. First, write a list of what really makes you happy. That could mean a lot of soul searching. Take your time putting this list together.

Your list could include these. Is it that five to ten minute quiet talk you have with God? Or is it a five to ten minute meditation just to calm you?

Maybe it's a walk just around the block or your property. How about just the one-on-one time with a loved one just to sit and talk about the hard stuff?

Remember the "No Regrets" part? Find the times to have those talks or walks so you don't have any regrets when those close to you are gone or when you are gone. What you may leave behind is a little peace with your loved ones.

> Remember the "No Regrets" part.

Chapter 4
Handling Complainers and Whiners

Do you ever have those days when you get to or have to deal with the people, whether co-workers or family members, who either complain or whine about *everything*!?

Well, it seems that this is what happens to me almost daily. I get frustrated to the point that I take on more work than I should, just so I don't have to deal with these characters. I know it's not healthy for me to constantly keep this up, and I know I should hold these people accountable for their actions when they affect others.

So, you and I must ask ourselves, "What do we do about it? Do we continue down this slow and painful destructive path, or do we take the time and breathe and stand our ground, and just say *no!*?"

I have come across complainers and whiners in my workplace through twenty-five years of federal service. No matter how much I try and help them see the right path, or try to figure out how to teach them or how to assist, they have this whining pattern down so well that nothing can change or improve with them.

So, while it seems that some of us have been doing a lot of self-changing lately, we feel at times that maybe, just maybe it's someone else's turn to change.

In a perfect world, or if I was Queen for a day and could wave my magic wand, I would make "no whining or complaining" happen. But, alas, I am not that good.

Take today for example: I had a co-worker who constantly complained about *everything*. Especially how everyone was out to make us look bad, saying others weren't working fast enough to put out the work orders like everyone should. This person was never happy and content, couldn't say a good word about anything.

Not too long ago I asked, "Just name me three good things about today." It didn't have to be anything about work; rather, just three things that were good about the day. Well, it was no shock to me that they had asked the same thing! So, I had to giggle, and I said, "First, I woke up today; second, I have a job, and third, I have a home and a safe place to lay my head at night."

Still this person wouldn't or couldn't respond with something positive. My point is this: we cannot change

Knowing You Have Done Your Best

everyone or anyone, and we are truly only in control of our actions and our feelings.

So when we come across complainers and whiners, my best advice is to take time, breathe, and ask these questions: "Am I contributing to the problem? Or am I going to be part of the solution and hold them accountable for their actions, and preserve my wellbeing?"

I choose to see situations clearly, exercise wisdom, and hold myself and others accountable when necessary and, most of all, protect my personal peace and wellbeing as well as foster an improved workplace atmosphere.

> We cannot change everyone or anyone, and we are truly only in control of our actions and our feelings.

Chapter 5
We Are All Extensions of God

In my view, the central issue for exercising personal faith may or may not be determined by attending or not attending church. Church attendance certainly *can* be part of searching for truth and finding it, and I readily admit I still am searching.

I would have to say, and I am sure you can find what little family I have left will also tell you, I am not much on going to church.

So, before you start preaching to me on if there is or is not a God, let me say why I choose not to attend.

Do I believe? Yes, I believe there is a Higher Power who drives and instructs us to do better, to find our way. Why do I go to church, or choose not to go?

Well, stated as sort of a simple answer: in the churches I have attended, I have found that their people, including leadership, tend to be judgmental, often behaving like hypocrites, and church has often become the worst place for me to try to find and encounter God. Unfortunately, it was where I encountered people who did not want to see and experience me as I really was, including struggles and all.

I was raised that when you attend church, women wear dresses and men wear slacks. Now I am not saying show up in ripped jeans or dirty clothes, *but* what if that kind of clothing was all an attender had? How one gets treated as you walk through the door sets a mood and sometimes causes a bad experience and negative memory that discourage people like me from continuing to attend.

I was raised to believe that God loves everyone, no matter what. His Son died for us so that we may live in His grace.

None of us can or will be perfect; we were not designed to be, and yet we search for God and how we can become more like Him. You and I know that self-will, doubt, and sometimes tough questions sort of put kinks in trying to be perfect in everything.

I quickly got tired of preachers standing at the pulpit telling me how I should or shouldn't live to be right with God, and yet I often found them doing the exact same things they told me not to do. What was my conclusion? "You can't have it both ways, people."

Knowing You Have Done Your Best

I thank God for the blessings He has given me every day, and throughout my whole life. I try my best daily not to judge people, but yet I still find a part of me that does judge.

I have come across people in my life who have helped me in my struggles with faith. They have helped me understand more, and given me answers to some of the misinterpretations I have had.

Again, we are back to taking small steps regularly. Maybe someday I will get back into going to church, or I may not, and then again, that is between me and God to decide.

Again, the central issue may not be just attending church, though it may include it.

You and I often hear people proclaim, "God does not put more on you than He knows you can handle." Well, I have a small issue with that statement. God is full of love and grace. Why would you or I even consider the thought that He puts anything negative on us purposefully? I don't believe He does.

I believe He is there through all the difficult times, no matter where they come from or what they entail. He hears and understands our pain and sorrow. He comforts us. That comfort and His love is where our inner strength comes from.

Just as if you were holding your own child, you express care, love, and you comfort them through a scraped knee or even the dreaded teen years when every day appears to be filled with drama for them. They pull their strength from you, and even though they might not see it, they will one day.

God's love for us is not just seen in church, though it can be. God's love is for you and me, regardless of circumstances, and faith, or the lack of it.

I am growing in my understanding, and seek Him more. Will you join me in this desire and quest? Maybe I'll even see you in church someday!

> God's love is for you and me, regardless of circumstances, and faith, or the lack of it.

Chapter 6
Face Changes for the Future

Changes for the future: they're inevitable. Does anyone really know what the future holds? Well, we would all like to think we have a handle on it, and maybe regarding parts of it, we do.

I was always so fearful when my husband, Butch, passed away that I was going to lose everything. By everything I am talking my home, at least. I wondered, "How was I going to handle all of this on my own?"

Now don't misunderstand me. I am a very independent person as most people who know me will tell you if you should happen to bump into any of them.

However, I have to say that the things I used to do on my own as an unmarried lady, I slowly started letting Butch deal with after marriage. This included tasks like mow the yard, change the oil in the car; you know, the responsibilities that had been labeled, "a man's job."

Now, here's a small back story. Before I met Butch, I worked for my family cleaning heavy equipment, like semi-trucks, log stackers, 950 forklifts, etc. So, I had to learn to drive and operate some of this heavy equipment.

Photo of Angela's dad washing a company truck, 1985
His business was S&S Steam Cleaning.

It was nothing for me to jump in a truck and drive it around the lot, back it up, and park it. But things changed when my mom and dad sold their business to my brother. I got away from doing that type of work.

Knowing You Have Done Your Best

Butch drove a truck for a living. It was a task he enjoyed, so it was nothing for him to pull our 28-ft. Fifth Wheel trailer around on trips and park it into camping spots.

Photo of Butch's truck taken by Butch in July, 1997
He worked on his truck and washed it every weekend.

I got comfortable with Butch doing what I didn't have to do anymore. Well, I sure was wrong about that!

Again, consider that "Face Changes for the Future" part.

My husband's given name was James Edward Williams. He was also known as Butch.

Photo of Butch, 1986, taken by his daughter, Teresa (Williams) Norris

All this time it never crossed my mind that I would lose my husband so fast. We often have this preconceived notion that a spouse will live to be in their 70s, 80s, or with extreme luck, into their 90s.

Knowing You Have Done Your Best

I was not expecting to lose him before his 62nd birthday.

Photo of Butch and Angela, February 14th Valentines Dance
Photography: Stray Angels Car Club, 1997

My future plans used to be that when he retired we were going to do more traveling and see some of the places we had always talked about. We would just pack up the camper and drive, or just jump in the car and go.

Pickup Truck and Camper
Photo taken by Butch in March, 2006

Well, my future suddenly changed when he passed. Since then I have found that I can stand on my own, even though that confidence was slow to come. I still have my house, and yes, I have re-learned how to back up my 28-ft. Fifth Wheel trailer. I can say this exercise was a little scary at first but also exciting at the same time. Now I feel more confident when I take the trailer on trips, and I can deal with whatever issues that may arise.

Knowing You Have Done Your Best

It has taken me long nine years to finally get to a point where I can feel good about myself again. I still have doubts about some things, but now it seems like a peace has come over me.

> I still have doubts about some things, but now it seems like a peace has come over me.

With my job every now and then, my employer will send me to acquire additional training at locations all across the country. This is the one and only time the government pays for a rental car in consideration of the airport where I land. There is no shuttle that can take me on the often hour-long drive needed to get to the training location.

I used to get so terrified that I would get lost, or I would dwell in fears of the unknown. There were many wild and crazy scenarios that would go through my mind.

One day as I was driving, it hit me. This calm peace washed over me. I thought, "If I have a tank full of gas, I *will* find my way."

This new-found peace gave me freedom and allowed me to be more open to reach new places and not be afraid to drive in big cities. I used to envy my aunt; she would travel to new places by herself, including other countries. The new and amazing experiences she has had! I hope I get to enjoy half of the brand new events she has ventured into, and start enjoying life more.

What I am trying to say is this: don't be afraid to take some chances, even if they are just small ones at first. Imagine how your world can be enriched by venturing out with even just small steps. You will probably grow more confident and maybe just a little more independent if you venture forth unafraid.

> I *will* find my way.

Talk about changing your future! Wow! The doors you could open or the ones you close may be those that are holding you back from moving forward or they may be barricades that are preventing you from healing.

You know the doors I am talking about: the doors that can cause you to harbor regrets like, "should've, would've, and could've." Those doors not only should be closed, but nailed shut, and never opened again.

> Don't be afraid to take some chances, even if they are just small ones at first. Imagine how your world can be enriched by venturing out with even just small steps.

Knowing You Have Done Your Best

Those doors never bring happiness. They box you in and promote your fears. They only bring sadness and regrets.

Those are the doors that keep you from moving forward and living your best possible life. Don't let them.

Chapter 7
Confronting Regrets

Now I can see those wheels in your head really spinning on this chapter, "Confronting Regrets." Even though I do not have any regrets with my loved ones who have passed, I do, however, have some regrets in my life as far as personal growth or career advancements are concerned. Like I often say, "I wish I hadn't passed up on that opportunity to go into the military, or passed up the chance for job advancement because I chose to stay in my town with my family versus leaving to a new area or state."

I should have pushed myself more. What I could have accomplished if I had taken a different path?

How often have you asked this question of yourself? So, this is where those "should've, would've, could've, and what ifs" start pulling you down.

I try every day to be thankful for what I have been blessed with: my daughter, my job, my home, and the ability to get up every day and put one foot in front of the other and just move through the day.

I love the old saying, "Have patience with me … God isn't finished with me yet." That is truer today more than it's ever been.

> I try every day to be thankful for what I have been blessed with.

I can see God sending all these angels to watch over me and they are tag-teaming because it is such big job. Now I must giggle. Those poor angels have truly earned their wings, that is for sure, and maybe they have received some hazard pay along the way or at the very least a month of paid vacation.

So, let's say you have some regrets in your life. Most people do.

The question is, "What do you do about them? Do you go on and on how about you wish you could have done it differently?"

> What do you do with your regrets?

Okay, now think about this. What if you just took all that energy and channeled it to something or someone which needs your focus right now? There are wants and needs you are likely uniquely gifted to fulfill. There are people you know who really need you.

Knowing You Have Done Your Best

Why do you continue wasting precious energy on dwelling on something in your past which you cannot change? Or, instead, do you stop the regrets and figure out how to get either a new dream or choose something as simple as not making the same decision that caused regret in the first place?

You alone make this choice for you.

Let those past decisions be reminders or stepping stones to bring about a learning experience. Refuse to consider failures that can bring about regret. Learn from your choices and make better ones.

> What if you just took all that energy and channeled it to something or someone that needs
> your focus right now?

Most of all choose to be thankful for yourself and all you have. An attitude of authentic and heartfelt thanksgiving can paint a whole new perspective for you.

> Stop the regrets and figure out how to get either a new dream or choose something as simple as not making the same decision that caused regret in the first place.

In my first years of employment, I often was required to interface with another employee who was quite difficult to work with. Let's just say that she was not one who tried to make anyone's job easier.

My job was to order supplies for our customers who were often disabled, and it was a job that was truly satisfying and rewarding.

> Choose to be thankful for yourself and all you have. An attitude of authentic and heartfelt thanksgiving can paint a whole new perspective for you.

I would serve many customers who would come in with the best attitude about their lives even though life may have dealt them a hard hand. Now some of these customers were not only disabled but in need of financial assistance as well. Wow! Talk about having a great sense of center or self-love.

This far-less-than-perfect employee was fond of repeatedly talking down to me and others, no matter the issue, and she did it in such a nice, yet sarcastic way. You know?

She was the kind of person who might wear a smile on her face and at the same time would try to convince you that you were the problem, or that you were not doing things right; she was never at fault. She possessed a critical and demeaning attitude. Yeah, she was one of those types.

Knowing You Have Done Your Best

Even now, after not having to deal with her for several years, I still am at a loss for words as to how to fully describe her, and get angry all over again thinking about it.

Anyway, back to my story ... Around the four-to-five year mark of working with her, I became so irritated and disgusted with her and her ways that it was affecting my ability to move on and accomplish much. I couldn't wait to get out of there, away from her negative influence.

Trust me when I say that upon leaving I sincerely missed the interactions with my needy customers day-to-day. They were special to me.

In my efforts to transition, I would apply for other jobs and be passed over, not because I was not qualified, but because of my attitude. I had let this other employee have control over my emotions, and to this day this is and always will be my biggest regret.

On second thought, instead of saying 'regret', how about we change it to *life lesson*? I like the sound of that better.

Through a series of events I was finally able to be moved out of that position to a new one. I was told at the time, "You didn't get the other jobs because you were unmarketable."

Talk about an eye-opener, and yes, my feelings were hurt. Then I had to take a step back and look at why I was "unmarketable."

I can't blame the lack of a better working condition. I can only blame myself for letting someone else have control over my emotions.

I don't like to use the word *hate*; it was more like extreme dislike, but to this day I still cannot get over the lingering and disgusting feelings I harbored for her. As you can see, I am still working on this collection of feelings, and not doing nearly as good a job at it as I would like, even years later. But I am working on it!

However, I try my best to not let negative feelings take over because that is an ugly and lonely road to go down. I know the feeling all too well of when you lose yourself and get caught up in the petty things that occur around you and you can't seem to break free.

> I can only blame myself for letting someone else have control over my emotions.

When regret strikes, you and I need to stop and take a moment and ask ourselves, "What can I do, or must I do to respond?"

Knowing You Have Done Your Best

Understand this question and its answer are not to foster revenge on someone else; rather, *this question and its answer are for our growth, self-protection, and preserving our God-given dignity. Our response is important: it will likely help us help others.*

I believe that developing and possessing a strong faith in yourself is a good way to start improving you, no matter if it is a long or short journey. Find your true self.

> I believe that developing and possessing a strong faith in yourself is a good way to start improving you, no matter if it is a long or short journey.
> Find your true self.

Begin your journey of self-discovery, even if you start with just one step. Begin with faith in you because you matter to God and others. And have faith in the God who gives you self-worth.

When you truly find you, you're probably in a far better position to help people who need your assistance and encouragement. There could be many.

Be strong for yourself *and* them.

Chapter 8
Forgiveness

Wow! This is a *powerful* word.

FORGIVENESS

Forgiveness can set you free is so many ways. Just think about it for a second. Consider a person who has hurt you, intentionally or unintentionally. You must find a way to forgive. Without forgiving, you are holding yourself back from becoming all you can be.

The weights will be lifted and you will find a release you have been looking for once you have forgiven that person and forgive yourself. Of course, you are allowed to possess and express emotions in the process, too, but not to your detriment.

Learning to forgive may be one of the hardest actions you will ever have to do. Think about the conditions or circumstances which brought you to the need to forgive in the first place. Pent-up anger is one. Betrayal is another.

If these are present within you, the anger and the bitterness that usually accompanies them will hold you back from achieving the freedom and release you are searching for.

Look at it this way. If you don't forgive those who have hurt you, they retain an unseen power over you. I am all for keeping the power of *my* emotions within me and not permitting other people to try and control that part of me.

You must find a way to get unhealthy feelings out and deal with them through the act of forgiving.

I can tell you this was not an easy road for me to go down.

> You must find a way to get unhealthy feelings out and deal with them through the act of forgiving.

I harbored a lot of angry feelings growing up. Tim, my brother, was the favorite in our family. Not only was he a *boy*, he was four years older than I, so he pretty much got away with a lot.

It took me several years to get beyond all that. It was devastating to me when my parents sold the business to him. When dad had first purchased the business, he did it so my brother could run it. Tim had 49% of the business and dad had 51%.

Knowing You Have Done Your Best

Tim ran the business for a few years, but not as successfully as our family desired. Not only did he put the business in debt, but Tim could not or would not give up his racing cars.

So dad took back the business and I took over. Hard work, careful planning, frugal spending, and effective operations became the name of the game. Not only did I get the business out of debt, but I got it paid off within two to three years.

Then one day my parents dropped the bomb. They told me they had sold it all to Tim. Needless to say, I was extremely hurt.

I felt all the old feelings come back of, "Yep, they love him more." I felt that I was and always would be a mistake to them. It seemed that no matter what I did it was never good enough. All that money coming in from all the jobs I worked to get that business debt paid off for almost a year was pure profit. I did not feel valued or appreciated.

I remember them saying to me after the fact, "We want to make sure you're okay." I smiled and looked at them and told them, "No, you're not concerned about me. Otherwise you would have not sold the business to Tim." Shortly thereafter I found a job and walked away from what I had worked so hard to earn.

Later, after my brother was killed, the business went to his brother-in-law. This was not the last time I was made to feel I didn't matter.

Earlier, my dad had experienced health issues, like having part of his foot amputated. The doctors would not allow him to come home until a ramp was built so he could have easy access to the house. He was going to be either riding a scooter or be in a wheelchair to get around until his foot healed.

So, it became the responsibility of Butch and me to install the ramp. We would go purchase all the materials to construct it. One day, as we were working on it, my mom stood outside watching us and said, "If Tim was still alive, this would have been done already."

The look on Butch's face hurt me more than any words my mom could have said. He stood up and looked at me because he knew her comment was uncalled for. He was about to tell her off but I gave him a look, pleading with him not to say anything. Mom just walked back into the house.

Butch looked and me and asked if I wanted to walk away. I told him no; I told him that I wanted to finish it and move on. You have to understand that by this time I was used to my mom saying things like that which were hurtful and not deserved.

Knowing You Have Done Your Best

The day my brother was killed I tried to console my parents, but they just pushed me away. To this day, because of the way my parents treated me, I still feel that maybe they thought it should have been me who died and not my brother.

I loved my parents, but it took a very long time to get over hurtful comments and an apparent lack of trust and confidence in me, especially on the heels of my rescuing the business and restoring it to a debt-free condition.

I now thank them for the way I was raised. Otherwise I would not been able to handle all that was put on me. But memories linger. I still struggle with some of the things that were either said or done to me. Though in my past they still come back to haunt my mind.

I have forgiven my parents. I believe they loved me. I think they knew somehow that I would be able to handle anything that might happen. I think they believed this to prepare me for a tougher life without them, and to this day I will always be grateful for their love.

It always seemed to me that I should have been born first, before my brother. The order of births always seemed backwards. I am still struggling with forgiving myself for my animosity toward my parents.

I have said before, "Have patience with me … God isn't finished with me yet." I am still in process. Most people are.

I do know this: there will be a day that I will forgive myself completely for my negative thoughts and feelings, and what a joyous day that is going to be! It is worth the effort I put forth to do what is right instead of what is wrong, regardless of how I may feel at the time.

> It is worth the effort I put forth to do what is right instead of what is wrong, regardless of how I may feel at the time.

I treasure some of the people who have crossed my path professionally. I am sincerely grateful for all the disabled veterans who have intersected my life while I worked to assist them. Now those are some amazing people who can forgive, and have done so.

I remember meeting a veteran who had been a prisoner of war. Talk about a grateful attitude: he offered forgiveness to the people who had held him captive. He chose to let go of all his anger and feelings of betrayal.

Wow! I am still impressed that he was able to move on and be thankful and not continue to live with hatred or suffer being debilitated with sadness. If this man can show forgiveness to the people that hurt him in war, which is far worse than anything I can imagine, I can show forgiveness to my parents and my brother and truly be grateful.

Knowing You Have Done Your Best

I choose to forgive for several reasons. First, it's a command of God. I'm forgiven; therefore, I choose to forgive others. Obedience to the command is for my wellbeing as well as for the wellbeing of persons who need my forgiveness. Plus, forgiving those who have caused me pain releases unnecessary weights on my shoulders. These shouldn't be mine to bear anyway.

> If this veteran could show forgiveness to the people that hurt him in war, which is far worse than anything I can imagine, I can show forgiveness to my parents and my brother and truly be grateful.

While memories may remain, with forgiveness the bitterness is gone. The memories and the people who have caused me pain no longer have power over me.

Forgiveness is release for me! It's good for all who do it and receive it, too.

Here is a Bible verse that reminds us to forgive.

Ephesians 4:32, New International Version (NIV):

> [32] Be kind and compassionate to one another, forgiving each other, just as in Christ God forgave you.

Bottom line:

FORGIVENESS WORKS.

Let me recommend that you access this website: https://www.crosswalk.com/faith/bible-study/what-does-the-bible-say-about-forgiveness.html

> Forgiveness is release for me! It's good for all who do it and receive it, too.

Chapter 9
Progress and Setbacks

There are going to be days when we all have setbacks. To this day I still endure times and memories that set me back to when all this started.

Writing this book, I was going through pictures and I found a photo album my mom had put together. I found pictures of my brother's truck accident.

Talk about a setback! Those pictures brought back some bad feelings that I thought I had dealt with long ago. How wrong I was on that!

It would be safe to say that my brother and I didn't always get along. I can remember a time when we went three whole years without talking to each other, even though we lived within five miles of each other.

We wouldn't spend Thanksgiving or Christmas at mom and dad's home like we used to. He would go on one day, and I would go a different day to see our parents. He made sure we were never in the same place at the same time.

Like all siblings, we had our issues. But I did get to see him one last time before he was killed.

Tim and his second wife had a baby boy and asked to borrow my rocking chair, so I took it to him. Tim was lying on the couch watching TV when I had brought the chair to him. He said maybe two or three words. It was obvious that he still didn't want to talk to me, so I got up, said good-bye, and left.

I believe that even if I knew or had some kind of guess that this was be the last time I saw him I am not sure it would have been any different.

I didn't know that just a few short days later he would be gone.

Seeing those old pictures caused one of my setbacks. I found a photo that showed my brother under a blanket, and I got angry all over again, not because of his death, however. It was a flash back of the feelings of, "It's all about him."

I had to stop and remind myself that this book was for me, not Tim. It also was not about my parents or even about Butch. This book is also written to encourage you.

As it is for many, my progress recovering from setbacks has been slow. I am sure that this is the way it should be.

Knowing You Have Done Your Best

We need time to absorb whatever life teachings come our way, lessons big and small. We are so used to instant gratification that we can lose the true meaning of important memories quickly.

> My progress recovering from setbacks has been slow. I am sure that this is the way it should be.

I believe that we can progress and overcome setbacks. To allow lessons to be truly meaningful, we need to take our time at a steady pace to process and learn. Striving to be sure we learn vital truths that life's events are teaching us, takes time.

> To allow lessons to be truly meaningful, we need to take our time at a steady pace to process and learn.

However, the truth is that the passage of time can be both a blessing and a curse when it comes to celebrating progress and processing setbacks. There are days that may seem that progress is never going to come, and then there are days where progress is happening so fast, it's hard to keep up with it.

It's difficult to imagine how much time has just flown by with all that has occurred, especially concerning the passing of loved ones.

Let me be vulnerable here. See if you can identify.

One day I may exist in a whirlwind of an emotional rollercoaster ride where it seems like I am falling in slow motion, and all of the memories of sad events flash in front of me and I cannot do anything to stop the ride.

But time also heals. Wow, look at me. I say this not arrogantly, but out of gratitude. Thankfully, I have made it through to the other side of grief and have been able to keep my sanity and make progress at the same time.

Yes, memories keep flooding back from time to time, but now, most days, they are happier memories. I try to not react to the sad memories that tend to cause setbacks because they are in the past and I don't benefit by dwelling on them.

If I dwell in past hurts and pain, this is when I allow progress to come to a halt. It's surely okay to work through those moments. The trick, as I have stated before, is to not dwell there for too long. I must learn and then move on.

Perhaps you experience this, too.

> If I dwell in past hurts and pain, this is when I allow progress to come to a halt ... I must learn and then move on.

Knowing You Have Done Your Best

The past teaches me valuable truths, and I embrace what I have learned. Then I let the sad memories go and leave them be.

It can be easier said than done. If you are like me, you must ask yourself, "How much do I care about my wellbeing?"

> If you are like me, you must ask yourself, "How much do I care about my wellbeing?"

Well, I choose to care more about myself now, more than I used to, that is for sure. I believe this good advice: never let go of your faith in you.

Believe in you, and grow with God. He loves you and cares for you. Be encouraged in this truth.

> Develop more faith in you with lots of God's help.
> *This is progress.*

Chapter 10
New Beginnings

We have come a long way on our journey to find our true focus, reach our real center, enjoy a peaceful feeling of meditation on life, and rest in God's peace. Hopefully we have forgiven ourselves and everyone one around us. What's next?

Well that would be a good question. The new beginning for you and me starts in *our* hearts and hands.

You have found you are worth all the work of enduring and learning you have done, and you and I will continue to believe and practice this.

> The new beginning for you and me starts in *our* hearts and hands.

What is my new beginning? Well, it's still "a work in progress," as they say. I am venturing out more, and I am doing some of the things that Butch and I always wanted to do but never found the time.

After nine years of being alone in the house, there is someone I have gotten close to, and I have to say it hasn't been an easy road to go down. However, he has helped me let go of some of the old feelings I have had that were holding me back.

Plus, I have taken on a few new projects around the house. For example, I have started building my dream kitchen on the deck since I have no room in the house. And I finally removed a 110-foot poplar tree that was in front of my house. I had been scared it was going to land either on the house or the road and hit some car or school bus that may just happen to be driving by.

It was a fear I conquered.

New beginnings can be scary and exciting at the same time. I try to focus more on the excitement of what is yet to come versus being scared to make any kind of movement at all.

> I conquered my fear and replaced it with positive action.

Being stuck in emotional states like grieving or anger is sometimes hard to overcome.

I feel at times it's such a waste of energy to relive the same old sad and painful emotions. Yet, we all have to go through the process of confronting pain if we want to deal with sad emotions.

The trick is to not stay in these emotions and the pain for too long. The longer we remain in the hurtful memories, the harder it becomes to overcome them.

Only you know when you have overstayed your welcome in that tough spot, and only you know when you have reached your limit.

Remember back to when I said, "small steps." Even one small step is the entrance to the new beginning. It's one step at a time. When you take it step by step, you'll find that each day gets a little easier in your desires to move forward.

> Only you know when you have overstayed your welcome in that tough spot, and only you know when you have reached your limit.

I clearly remember my cousin talking to me a few months after Butch had passed. He said, "It will get easier." He had lost his wife a few years earlier. I looked at him and told him, "I don't know how." All he did was smile at me and said, "You will find your way."

Well, he was right. I have slowly found my way to a happier and more productive place in my life. I believe that with a little self-love and reliance upon God, anyone can get to their life's new beginning.

I believe that life's new beginnings have a lot to do with having few or no regrets, knowing you have done your best. These kinds of positive perspectives make it more possible to enter into the faith you and I need, and have been searching for.

We can exercise this faith and demonstrate confidence in us, through our faith in God.

"Faith" is another powerful word for me. It simply is a part of my life.

What is faith? It is belief in something we may not be able to see or touch. But we have this faith because of the evidence that God loves us.

Here is a scripture where faith and evidence are connected. In fact, I believe they are never separated.

Hebrews 11:1 (KJV):

Now faith is the substance of things hoped for, the evidence of things not seen.

Knowing You Have Done Your Best

Feelings may be altogether different than faith.

You and I might experience feelings or emotions we treasure deep inside because we are convinced that something, or Someone, is protecting us and helping us move forward.

Feelings, like faith, are emotions we cannot touch or see, but we know they are present. So, why do some believe in "feelings" but question a belief in God?

Faith and feelings, when we are dependent upon God, can be strongly connected, but faith is primary.

That is probably another discussion for another day. We could spend several days on that subject.

For me, it's my desire to grow to a higher level of faith, including my feelings of thankfulness. This perspective keeps me moving forward, learning the lessons of life, and convinces me to truly possess no regrets, knowing I have done my best.

> It's my desire to grow to a higher level of faith, including my feelings of thankfulness.

Closing Thoughts

Strength can be like a large rock, immovable. We chose the cover image for a reason. While my resolve is strong, I realize that God is my source. He also plans my course. I trust Him. Though surrounded by water the rock remains standing, strong and sure.

Nowhere in this book have I decided or declared that apart from Him I can make it on my own.

However, I value the strength of determination to not allow difficulties of the past to rule my present.

I desire to learn from the past but not dwell there, and I choose to forgive and be thankful.

Perhaps these are your desires, too.

This book was put together to tell my story, true. It was also written to let you know that forgiveness, faith in God, a growing confidence in yourself, and strong desires can help you and I overcome any of life's sorrows, setbacks, sadness, and disappointments, no matter whether they make themselves known in personal or work environments.

Closing Thoughts

I believe we can experience encouragement from true friends and an immovable confidence in God, while we constantly desire and strive for greater understanding and a stronger faith.

Remember what I said before: "Have patience with me ... God isn't finished with me yet."

God shows us that although sorrows will come, there is more to life than dwelling in grief. We have hope because of Him. He accepts us as we are and helps us mature through what we learn. It's a process of growth.

Daily life presents us all with constant opportunities to mature and experience more. I choose growth and not stagnation. I choose to learn from the past and move on to the future with a stronger faith in the Rock who is God.

Perhaps you are walking this journey, like I have been. Remember, it is one step at a time.

If your experience is similar to mine, you may experience setbacks along with progress, but when you trust God, He will never let you down.

That is my experience. I believe it can be yours, too. I believe that you, too, can know you have done your best, with no regrets.

Credits in Order of Appearance

Chapter 1
Events and How They Were Handled

Photo of the Cross nailed to the tree near to the location where Angela's brother was killed on October 19, 1992

Photo of Angela's family taken September, 1979

"Saying Good-bye to a Lot of Anger" The Chair Bonfire Photo taken by the author, November 27, 2016

Chapter 2
Care for the Poor and Disadvantaged
    One Small Step (poem)

Chapter 6
Face Changes for the Future

Photo of Angela's dad washing a company truck, 1985 His business was S&S Steam Cleaning.

Photo of Butch's truck taken by Butch in July, 1997

Credits In Order of Appearance

Photo of Butch, 1986, taken by his daughter, Teresa (Williams) Norris

Photo of Butch and Angela, February 14th Valentines Dance Photography: Stray Angels Car Club, 1997

Photo of Pickup Truck and Camper
Photo taken by Butch in March, 2006

Chapter 8
Forgiveness

Scripture quotation: Ephesians 4:32, **New International Version (NIV)** *Holy Bible*, New International Version ®, NIV ® Copyright ©1973, 1978, 1984, 2011 by Biblica, Inc. ® Used by permission. All rights reserved worldwide.

Website recommendation by the author:
https://www.crosswalk.com/faith/bible-study/what-does-the-bible-say-about-forgiveness.html

Chapter 10
New Beginnings

Scripture quotation: Hebrews 11:1, **King James Version (KJV)**, *The Holy Bible*, Public Domain.

Appreciation

I want to give a shout out to my true friends who have encouraged me throughout these years of adjustment, pushing me to try new adventures and keep believing. These friendships are uplifting to a stronger measure than I can adequately express. To all of you: *thank you*.

And special appreciation goes to my daughter, Jessica, who is the center of my world. Through her example I truly have begun to know the meaning of unconditional love.

I want to say a heartfelt thank you to Randy Beck, **www.mydomaintools.com** for designing my website, and the great talks we have had. He is truly a new friend I have gained.

Let me also say a thank you to Glen Aubrey and his team for the constant encouragement and guidance throughout the process of writing this book. Without Glen and **Creative Team Publishing (CTP),** this book would not have been written. Please see **www.CreativeTeamPublishing.com.**

Products and Resources

To Order additional copies of this book please visit the book's website:

www.KnowingYouHaveDoneYourBest.com

Additional resources:

These organizations help people find food banks, rescue missions, and homeless shelters in their areas.

FEEDING AMERICA:
https://www.feedingamerica.org/find-your-local-foodbank

RESCUE MISSION ALLIANCE:
https://www.erescuemission.org/

EMERGENCY and HOMELESS SHELTERS:
https://www.211unitedway.org/search-category/emergency-and-homeless-shelters/

The Author

Angela Williams is your average working woman, daughter, mom, wife, and friend. She, like all of us, has suffered through an ebb and flow of life and found herself at the end of a tight rope. However, she has found the strength and determination to make the best choices in those moments and follow through with vigor.

This is her first book. Encouraged by friends and family, she decided to tell her story in hopes that is finds its way into familiar places among its readers. She wanted to remind everyone who thumbed through these pages that no matter how dire life may seem, how fleeting every passing day may appear, there should be no regrets in our choices as long as these are choices we follow through with.

She reminds us that everyone is human and in one way or another has already gone through or will go through tough times. All of us will have to make the best possible decisions to overcome them.

~Jessica Stafford, August, 2019

CPSIA information can be obtained
at www.ICGtesting.com
Printed in the USA
BVHW031634211019
561663BV00001B/155/P